TAO
OF STO
STO
TE CHING

A Daily Doodah

Spring

BANYA PRESS

Montreal · Denver · San Francisco · Los Angeles

For permission requests, contact the publisher:
www.banyapress.com

To translate this legalese into Spanglish, contact Juan:
www.banyapress.com

ISBN: 979-8-9941701-1-3
Printed in the United States of America
First Edition

Compiled by Anonymous Sauna
Design by Robert Van Horne
Illustrations by Gabriel Gigliotti

Classical texts from the Tao Te Ching and the Stoic authors used in this volume are in the public domain; arrangement and presentation are original to this edition.

10 9 8 7 6 5 4 3 2 1

RANDALL: LISTEN, DO YOU WANT TO
RUN THIS GANG?

STRUTTER: NO...NO... WE AGREED...
NO LEADER.

RANDALL: RIGHT! SO SHUT UP AND DO
AS I SAY.

— TIME BANDITS

INTRODUCTION

Over the years, Taoist and Stoic philosophy have become some of our most reliable therapeutic tools—clean, unsentimental, and strangely kind. They never try to fix you. They just point toward reality and ask whether you're willing to stop resisting it—if only for a minute. Both traditions grasp something modern culture forgets: that growth is cyclical, not linear. Sometimes the work is doing. Sometimes the work is waiting. In the rooms where we meet our therapy clients, these ideas show up less as abstract concepts and more as everyday companions—ways of sitting with grief, confusion, and change without turning away.

This spring edition turns toward that truth. Spring isn't about pulling blossoms out of the frozen earth. It's about thawing, softening, and letting what slept through winter awaken in its own time. The Tao speaks of returning. The Stoics speak of accepting what is. Spring lives right at the intersection of both: life reemerging without asking for permission. Sometimes the work is simply letting yourself be seen by another person long enough to notice that you're changing.

The creators of this book designed it to be read in a sauna because heat accelerates honesty, and sweat makes philosophers of us all. Pairing that heat with a cold plunge can make you feel like you're dying and resurrecting yourself.

Once, after staying too long in a sauna late one winter night,
we got so overheated that we panicked, ran to a frozen pond
nearby, broke a hole in the ice with the oar of an old rowboat,
and jumped in. It was terrifying. It was clarifying. We lived.
Spring feels like that, too: shock, renewal, breath returning.

You don't have to read this in a sauna, of course. If sweating
isn't your thing, that's fine. Read it in bed, on the subway,
on a park bench, or near an open window. The point isn't
the heat—it's the pause. That rare moment when your nervous
system loosens its grip and you remember what ease feels like.

Short Taoist and Stoic reflections. Simple illustrations that
invite you to engage, or not. No explanation, moralizing, or
agenda. Just something to reach for whenever you have a quiet
moment to yourself. You don't have to make anything happen.
Spring already knows what it's doing. So do the deeper parts
of you that keep finding their way back to the light—no matter
how many winters you've been through.

Christopher Mooney, LCSW & Kenyon Phillips, LMSW
Founders, Lumen Therapy Collective
Spring 2026

TAOIST

STOIC

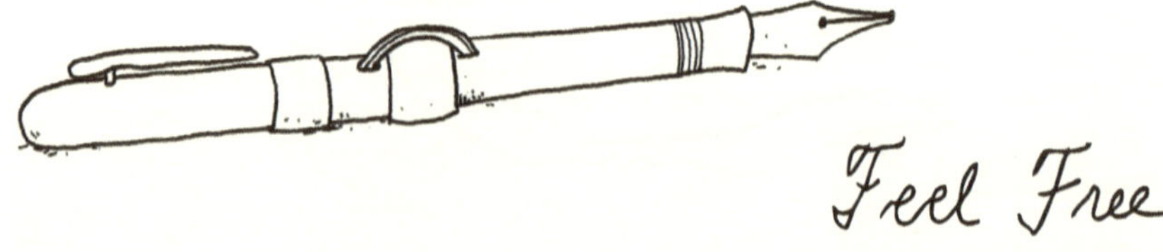

INSTRUCTIONS

This is a seasonal daily reader.
Or is it?

Each day provides a complete protein—
a Stoic morsel paired with a soupçon of the Tao Te Ching—
served with an illustration garnish.

The suggested use case is between
one and one hundred pages per day.

Attend to the words.
Drift over to the illustration.
Mosey on back to the words.
What stirs within? What tingles without?

You'll notice generous white space throughout the book.
Use it freely:
write notes, draw arrows, underline aggressively, sketch poorly,
wipe boogers, wipe the slate clean.

If you're reading in a sauna,
aim perspiration droplets
into the ample margins.

The book does not mind.
Neither do the Stoics.
The Tao has already moved on.

APRIL

Strength

"Can you remain tranquil until
 right action occurs by itself?"

— Lao Tzu, 15

"How easy it is to repel and to wipe away every
 impression which is troublesome or unsuitable,
 and immediately to be in all tranquility."

— Marcus Aurelius, *Meditations 5.2*

TAO

"By knowing the constant we can accept things
as they are. By accepting things as they are,
we become impartial. By being impartial,
we become one with Heaven. By being one
with Heaven, we become one with the Tao."

— Lao Tzu, 16

STO

"Nothing happens to any man which he is not
formed by nature to bear."

— Marcus Aurelius, *Meditations 5.17*

"The Master puts herself last, and finds herself in the place of authority. She detaches herself from all things; therefore she is united with all things. She gives no thought to self. She is perfectly fulfilled."

— Lao Tzu, 7

"If wisdom were given me under the express condition that it must be kept hidden and not uttered, I should refuse it. No good thing is pleasant to possess without friends to share it."

— Seneca, *Letters, 6.4*

"Can you focus your life-breath until you become
supple as a newborn child? While you cleanse
your inner vision, will you be found without fault?
Can you love people and lead them without
forcing your will on them?"

— Lao Tzu, 10

"Withdraw into yourself, as far as you can.
Associate with those who will make a better man of you.
Welcome those whom you yourself can improve.
The process is mutual; for men learn while they teach."

— Seneca, *Letters, 7.8*

"To understand the small is called clarity.
Knowing how to yield is called strength.
To use your inner light for understanding regardless
of the danger is called depending on the Constant."

— Lao Tzu, 52

"Attend to the matter which is before thee,
whether it is an opinion or an act or a word."

— Marcus Aurelius, *Meditations 8.23*

"Preferring simplicity and freedom from desires,
avoiding the pitfalls of knowledge and wrong action.
For those who practice not-doing,
everything will fall into place."

— Lao Tzu, 3

"Those who seem to be busied with nothing are busied
with the greater tasks; they are dealing at the same time
with things mortal and things immortal."

— Seneca, *Letters* 8.6

"When Heaven gives and takes away, can you be content
with the outcome? When you understand all things,
can you step back from your own understanding?"

— Lao Tzu, 10

"Wilt thou too then be made a fool for these things?
I was once a fortunate man, but I lost it, I know not how.
But fortunate means that a man has assigned to himself
a good fortune: and a good fortune is good disposition
of the soul, good emotions, good actions."

— Marcus Aurelius, *Meditations 5.36*

"All of creation is born from substance.
 Substance is born of nothing-ness."

— Lao Tzu, 40

"He who reposes should act and he who acts should take
repose. Discuss the problem with Nature; she will tell
you that she has created both day and night."

— Seneca, *Letters*, 3.6

TAO

"When you have accomplished your goal
  simply walk away.
  This is the path to Heaven."

— Lao Tzu, 9

STO

"As a horse when he has run, a dog when he has
  tracked the game, a bee when it has made the honey,
  so a man when he has done a good act does not call out
  for others to come and see, but he goes on to another act,
  as a vine goes on to produce again the grapes in season."

— Marcus Aurelius, *Meditations, 5.6*

"Because the master isn't self centered, people can see
the light in her. Because she does not boast of herself,
she becomes a shining example. Because she does
not glorify herself, she becomes a person of merit.
Because she wants nothing from the world,
the world can not overcome her."

— Lao Tzu, 22

"This too is a property of the rational soul,
love of one's neighbour, and truth and modesty,
and to value nothing more than itself, which is also
the property of Law. Thus right reason differs
not at all from the reason of justice."

— Marcus Aurelius, *Meditations, 11.1*

TAO

"Thus the Master is willing to help everyone,
  and doesn't know the meaning of rejection.
  She is there to help all of creation, and doesn't
  abandon even the smallest creature.
  This is called embracing the light."

— Lao Tzu, 27

STO

"About what am I now employing my own soul?
  On every occasion I must ask myself this question,
  and inquire, what have I now in this part of me
  which they call the ruling principle?
  And whose soul have I now?
  That of a child, or of a young man,
  or of a feeble woman, or of a tyrant,
  or of a domestic animal, or of a wild beast?"

— Marcus Aurelius, *Meditations, 5.11*

"Know the honorable, but do not shun the disgraced:
embrace the world as it is. If you embrace the world
with compassion, then your virtue will return you
to the uncarved block."

— Lao Tzu, 28

"One man is not miserable through the means of another."

— Epictetus, *Discourses, Book 1, 9.7*

"Watch the workings of all of creation, but contemplate
their return to the source. All creatures in the universe
return to the point where they began. Returning to
the source is tranquility because we submit to Heaven's
design. Returning to Heaven's design is called being
constant. Knowing the constant is called 'enlightenment'."

— Lao Tzu, 16

"Think of the universal substance, of which thou
hast a very small portion; and of universal time,
of which a short and indivisible interval has been
assigned to thee; and of that which is fixed by destiny,
and how small a part of it thou art."

— Marcus Aurelius, *Meditations, 5.23*

TAO

"If you fail to honor your teacher or fail to enjoy your
  student, you will become deluded no matter how smart
  you are. It is the secret of prime importance."

— Lao Tzu, 27

STO

"Art thou angry with him whose armpits stink?
Art thou angry with him whose mouth smells foul?
What good will this danger do thee? He has such a
mouth, he has such arm-pits: it is necessary that such
an emanation must come from such things -but the man
has reason, it will be said, and he is able, if he takes
pain, to discover wherein he offends - I wish thee well
of thy discovery. Well then, and thou hast reason: by thy
rational faculty stir up his rational faculty; show him
his error, admonish him. For if he listens,
thou wilt cure him, and there is no need of anger."

— Marcus Aurelius, *Meditations*, 5.27

"The highest good is not to seek to do good,
 but to allow yourself to become it."

— Lao Tzu, 38

"The way is long if one follows precepts,
 but short and helpful if one follows patterns."

— Seneca, *Letters 6.5*

"The sages of old were as careful as someone crossing a
frozen stream in winter. Alert as if surrounded
on all sides by the enemy. Courteous as a guest.
Fluid as melting ice. Whole as an uncarved block of wood.
Receptive as a valley. Cloudy as muddy water."

— Lao Tzu, 15

"Epicurus counseled:
Cherish some man of high character,
and keep him ever before your eyes, living
as if he were watching you, and ordering
all your actions as if he beheld them."

— Seneca, *Letters 11.8*

"Only when there is no competition
 will we all live in peace."

— Lao Tzu, 8

"Change the age in which you live, and you have too much.
 But in every age, what is enough remains the same."

— Seneca, *Letters 17.10*

WHAT'S WRONG?
I'VE FAILED TO ASCEND THE STATUS HIERARCHY

"One who is filled with the Tao is like a newborn child."

— Lao Tzu, 55

"Thy present opinion founded on understanding,
and thy present conduct directed to social good,
and thy present disposition of contentment with
everything which happens – that is enough."

— Marcus Aurelius, *Meditations, 9.6*

"To excessively attempt to extend life is not appropriate.
To try and alter the life-breath is unnatural.
The master understands that when something
reaches its prime it will soon begin to decline.
Changing the natural is against the way of the Tao.
Those who do it will come to an early end."

— Lao Tzu, 56

"To children who put their hand into a narrow-necked
earthen vessel and bring out figs and nuts, this happens;
if they fill the hand, they cannot take it out, and then
they cry. Drop a few of them and you will draw things out."

— Epictetus, *Discourses 3.9.21*

"The Master doesn't seek fulfillment.
 Only those who are not full are able to be used.
 This brings the feeling of completeness."

— Lao Tzu, 15

"Wisdom offers wealth in ready money,
 and pays it over to those in whose eyes
 she has made wealth superfluous."

— Seneca, *Letters 17.10*

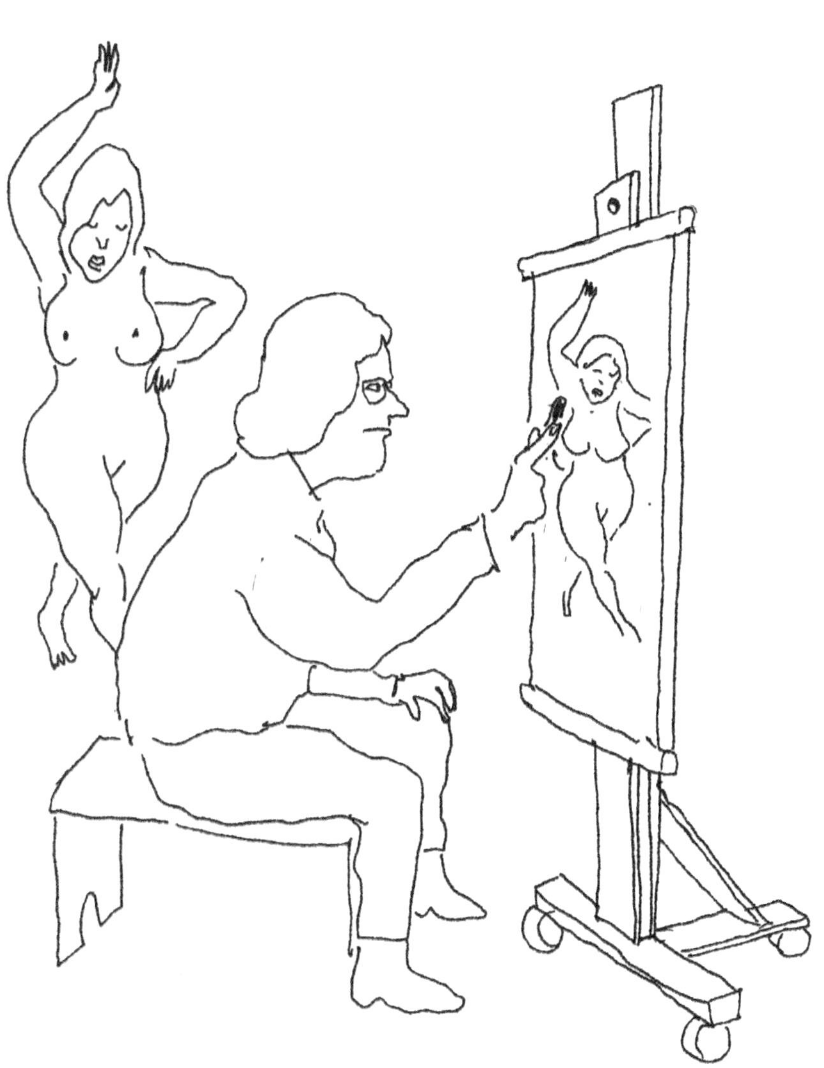

TAO

"The Master does not force virtue on others,
thus she is able to accomplish her task.
The ordinary person who uses force, will find
that they accomplish nothing."

— Lao Tzu, 38

STO

"One man, when he has done a service to another,
is ready to set it down to his account as a favour conferred.
Another is not ready to do this, but still in his own mind
he thinks of the man as his debtor, and he knows what
he has done. A third in a manner does not even know
what he has done, but he is like a vine which has
produced grapes, and seeks for nothing more
after it has once produced its proper fruit."

— Marcus Aurelius, *Meditations*, 5.6

"The masters of old attained unity with the Tao.
Heaven attained unity and became pure.
The earth attained unity and found peace.
The spirits attained unity so they could minister.
The valleys attained unity that they might be full.
Humanity attained unity that they might flourish.
Their leaders attained unity that they might set the
example. This is the power of unity."

— Lao Tzu, 38

"For two reasons it is right to be content with that which
happens to thee; the one, because it was done for thee
and prescribed for thee, and in a manner had reference
to thee, originally from the most ancient causes spun
with thy destiny; and the other, because even that which
comes severally to every man is to the power which
administers the universe a cause of felicity and
perfection, nay even of its very continuance."

— Marcus Aurelius, *Meditations*, 5.8

TAO

"Where there is music and good food,
  people will stop to enjoy it. But words spoken
  of the Tao seem to them boring and stale.
  When looked at, there is nothing for them to see.
  When listened for, there is nothing for them to hear.
  Yet if they put it to use, it would never be exhausted."

— Lao Tzu, 35

STO

"How comforting it is to have tired out one's appetites, and
  to have done with them!"

— Seneca, *Letters 12.5*

"Keep your mouth closed and embrace a simple life,
  and you will live care-free until the end of your days.
  If you try to talk your way into a better life,
  there will be no end to your trouble."

— Lao Tzu, 52

"Do me the favour, when men surround you and
  try to talk you into believing that you are unhappy,
  to consider not what you hear but what you yourself
  feel, and to take counsel with your feelings and question
  yourself independently, because you know your own
  affairs better than anyone else does."

— Seneca, *Letters* 13.6

"Knowing you don't know is wholeness.
Thinking you know is a disease.
Only by recognizing that you have an illness
can you move to seek a cure."

— Lao Tzu, 71

"Some things torment us more than they ought;
some torment us before they ought; and some
torment us when they ought not to torment us at all.
We are in the habit of exaggerating, or imagining,
or anticipating, sorrow."

— Seneca, *Letters* 13.5

"Those who are stiff and rigid are the disciple of death.
Those who are soft and yielding are the disciples of life.
The rigid and stiff will be broken.
The soft and yielding will overcome."

— Lao Tzu, 76

"Increase and beautify the good that is in you."

— Seneca, *Letters 13.15*

SPIDER-MAN

"The Master desires no possessions. Since the things
she does are for the people, she has more than she needs.
The more she gives to others, the more she has for herself."

— Lao Tzu, 81

"How pleasant it is to demand nothing; how noble it is
to be contented and not to be dependent upon Fortune."

— Seneca, *Letters 15.9*

"When a superior person hears of the Tao,
  she practices it diligently. When an average person
  hears of the Tao, he believes half of it, and doubts
  the other half. When a foolish person hears
  of the Tao, he laughs out loud. If he didn't laugh,
  it wouldn't be the Tao."

— Lao Tzu, 41

"Thou hast leisure or ability to check arrogance:
  thou hast leisure to be superior to pleasure and pain:
  thou hast leisure to be superior to love of fame,
  and not to be vexed at stupid and ungrateful people,
  nay even to care for them."

— Marcus Aurelius, *Meditations 8.8*

"The Tao hides in the unnamed,
 yet it alone nourishes and completes all things."

— Lao Tzu, 41

"Am I doing anything? I do it with reference to the good
 of mankind. Does anything happen to me? I receive it
 and refer it to the gods, and the source of all things,
 from which all that happens is derived."

— Marcus Aurelius, *Meditations 8.25*

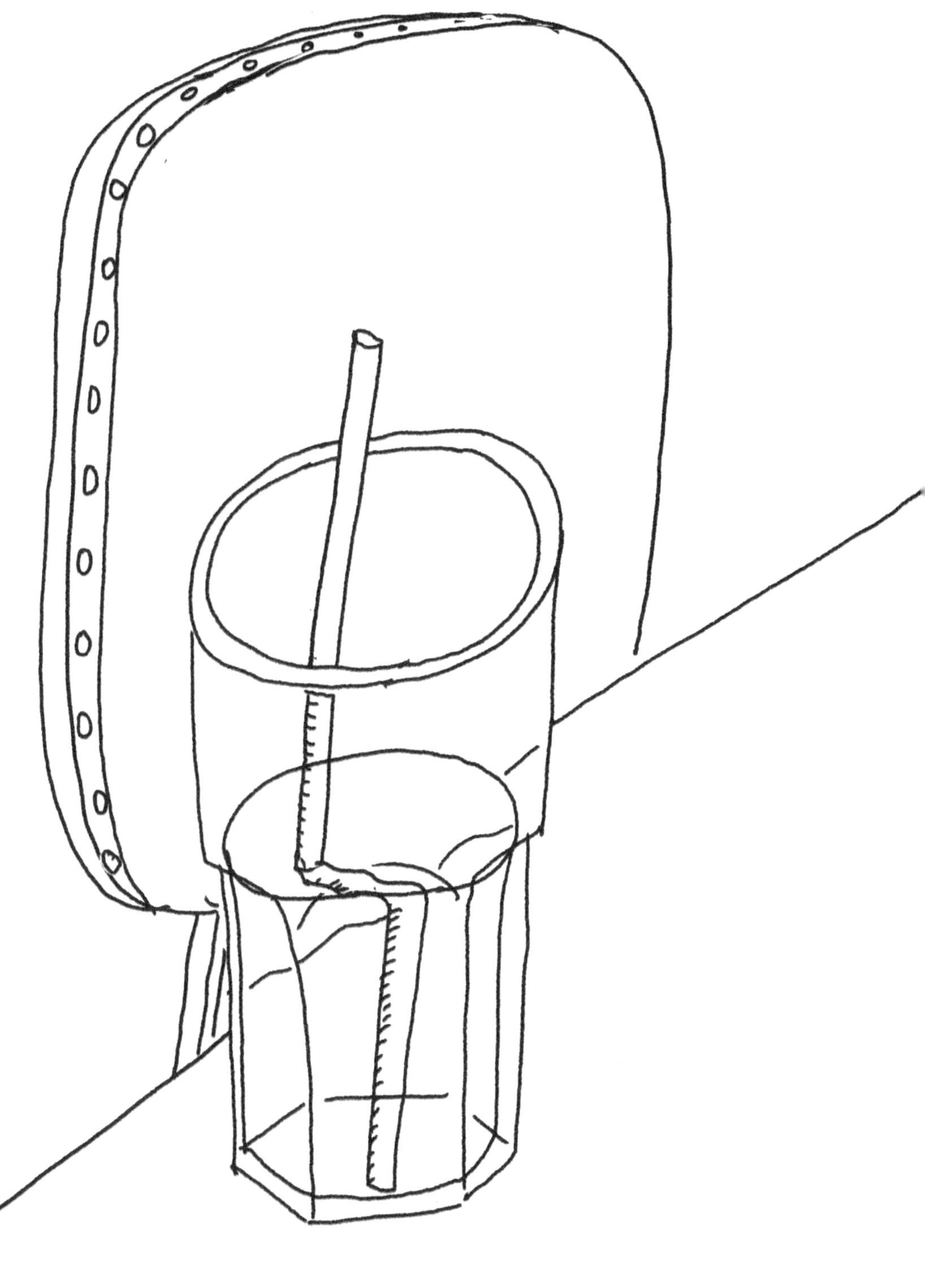

TAO

"The great Tao flows unobstructed in every direction.
 All things rely on it to conceive and be born,
 and it does not deny even the smallest of creation.
 When it has accomplished great wonders,
 it does not claim them for itself."

— Lao Tzu, 34

STO

"A man's peace of mind does not depend upon Fortune;
 for, even when angry She grants enough for our needs."

— Seneca, *Letters 18.7*

MAY

Balance

"The Master acts on what she feels and not what she sees.
She shuns the latter and prefers to seek the former."

— Lao Tzu, 12

"And consider this which is near to thee, this boundless
abyss of the past and of the future in which all things
disappear. How then is he not a fool who is puffed up
with such things or plagued about them and makes
himself miserable? For they vex him only for a time,
and a short time."

— Marcus Aurelius, *Meditations, 5.22*

"Do you want to rule the world and control it?
 I don't think it can ever be done."

— Lao Tzu, 29

"Do you not rather thank the gods that they have allowed
you to be above these things which they have not placed
in your power, and have made you accountable only for
those which are in your power?"

— Epictetus, *Discourses, Book 1, 12.5*

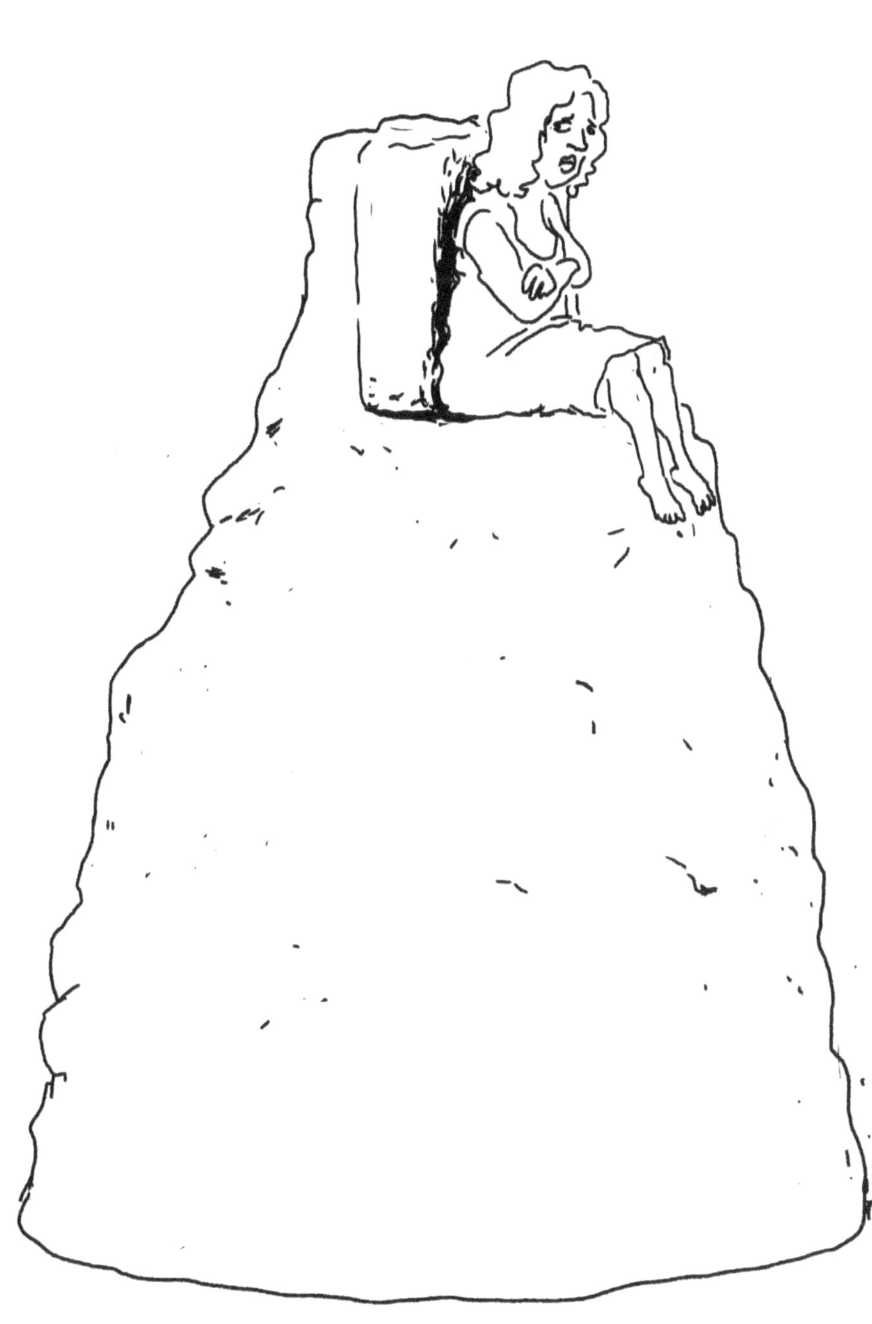

"Nurture the darkness of your soul until you become whole."

— Lao Tzu, 10

"When then you have shut the doors and made darkness
within, remember never to say that you are alone,
for you are not; but God is within, and your Daemon*
is within, and what need have they of light to see
what you are doing?"

*For the Stoics, a *daemon* is best understood as an *inner guiding principle*.

— Epictetus, *Discourses, Book 1, 12.5*

"Success is as dangerous as failure, and we are often
our own worst enemy. What does it mean that success
is as dangerous as failure? He who is superior is also
someone's subordinate. Receiving favor and losing it
both cause alarm. What does it mean that we are often
our own worst enemy? The reason I have an enemy is
because I have a "self". If I no longer had a "self",
I would no longer have an enemy."

— Lao Tzu, 13

"That which shakes us most is the dread which
hangs over us from our neighbour's ascendancy;
for it is accompanied by great outcry and uproar."

— Seneca, *Letters 14.4*

"Being one with Tao, we are no longer concerned about
losing our life because we know the Tao is constant
and we are one with Tao."

— Lao Tzu, 16

"The fool's life is empty of gratitude and full of fears;
its course lies wholly toward the future."

— Seneca, *Letters 15.9*

"Why do we humans go on endlessly about little when
nature does much in a little time? If you open yourself
to the Tao, you and Tao become one."

— Lao Tzu, 23

"If you live according to nature, you will never be poor;
if you live according to opinion, you will never be rich."

— Epicurus as quoted by Seneca, *Letters 16.7*

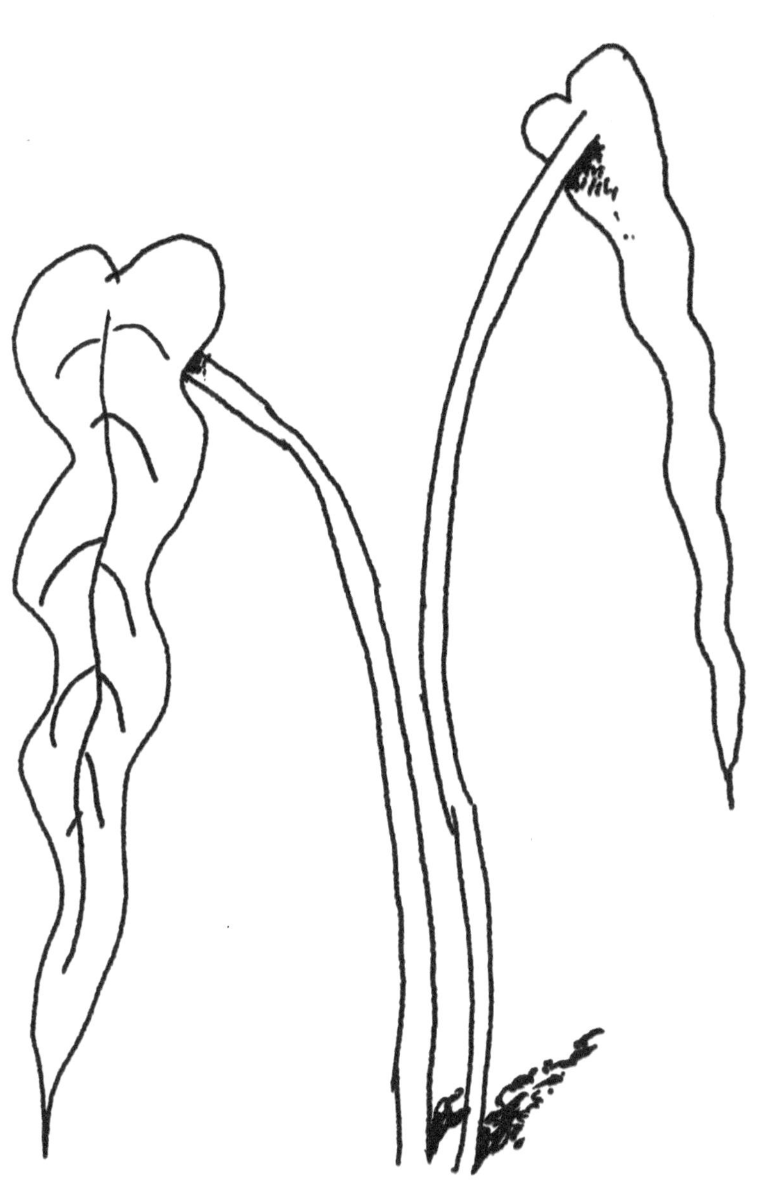

"People despise being orphaned, widowed and poor.
But the noble ones take these as their titles.
In losing, much is gained, and in gaining, much is lost."

— Lao Tzu, 42

"Suppose that the property of many millionaires is heaped
up in your possession. Assume that fortune carries you far
beyond the limits of a private income, decks you with gold,
clothes you in purple, and brings you to such a degree of
luxury and wealth that you can bury the earth under your
marble floors; that you may not only possess, but tread
upon, riches. Add statues, paintings, and whatever any
art has devised for the satisfaction of luxury; you will only
learn from such things to crave still greater."

— Seneca, *Letters 16.8*

"The master says:
I do not meddle in their personal lives,
and the people become prosperous.
I let go of all my desires, and the people
return to the Uncarved Block."

— Lao Tzu, 57

"Thou canst pass thy life in an equable flow of happiness,
if thou canst go by the right way, and think and act
in the right way...and to hold good to consist in the
disposition to justice and the practice of it, and in this
to let thy desire find its termination."

— Marcus Aurelius, *Meditations, 5.35*

"Therefore the Master lets things take their course
and thus never fails. She doesn't hold on to things
and never loses them. By pursuing your goals
too relentlessly, you let them slip away."

— Lao Tzu, 64

"Why then do you draw on yourself the things
for which you are not responsible?
It is, indeed, a giving of trouble to yourself."

— Epictetus, *Discourses, Book 1, 12.5*

"A virtuous person will do the right thing,
 and persons with no virtue will take advantage of others.
 The Tao does not choose sides.
 The good person receives from the Tao
 because she is on its side."

— Lao Tzu, 64

"If you choose to be modest and faithful,
 who shall not allow you to be so?"

— Epictetus, *Discourses, Book 2, 2.1*

"The Tao of Heaven nourishes by not forcing.
 The Tao of the Wise person acts by not competing."

— Lao Tzu, 81

"There is great pleasure, not only in maintaining old
and established friendships, but also in beginning
and acquiring new ones."

— Seneca, *Letters 9.6*

"Why should the lord of a thousand chariots be amused
at the foolishness of the world? If you abandon yourself
to foolishness, you lose touch with your beginnings.
If you let yourself become distracted, you will lose
the basis of your power."

— Lao Tzu, 26

"Some things torment us more than they ought;
some torment us before they ought; and some
torment us when they ought not to torment us at all.
We are in the habit of exaggerating, or imagining,
or anticipating, sorrow."

— Seneca, *Letters 13.5*

TAO

"Less and less remains until you arrive at non-action.
 When you arrive at non-action,
  nothing will be left undone."

— Lao Tzu, 48

STO

"Let us cherish and love old age; for it is full of pleasure
 if one knows how to use it."

— Seneca, *Letters 12.4*

"Know the white, yet keep to the black: be a model
for the world. If you are a model for the world,
the Tao inside you will strengthen and you will
return whole to your eternal beginning."

— Lao Tzu, 28

"What pleased me to-day in the writings of Hecato...
'What progress, you ask, have I made? I have begun
to be a friend to myself.' That was indeed a great benefit;
such a person can never be alone. You may be sure
that such a man is a friend to all mankind."

— Seneca, *Letters 6.7*

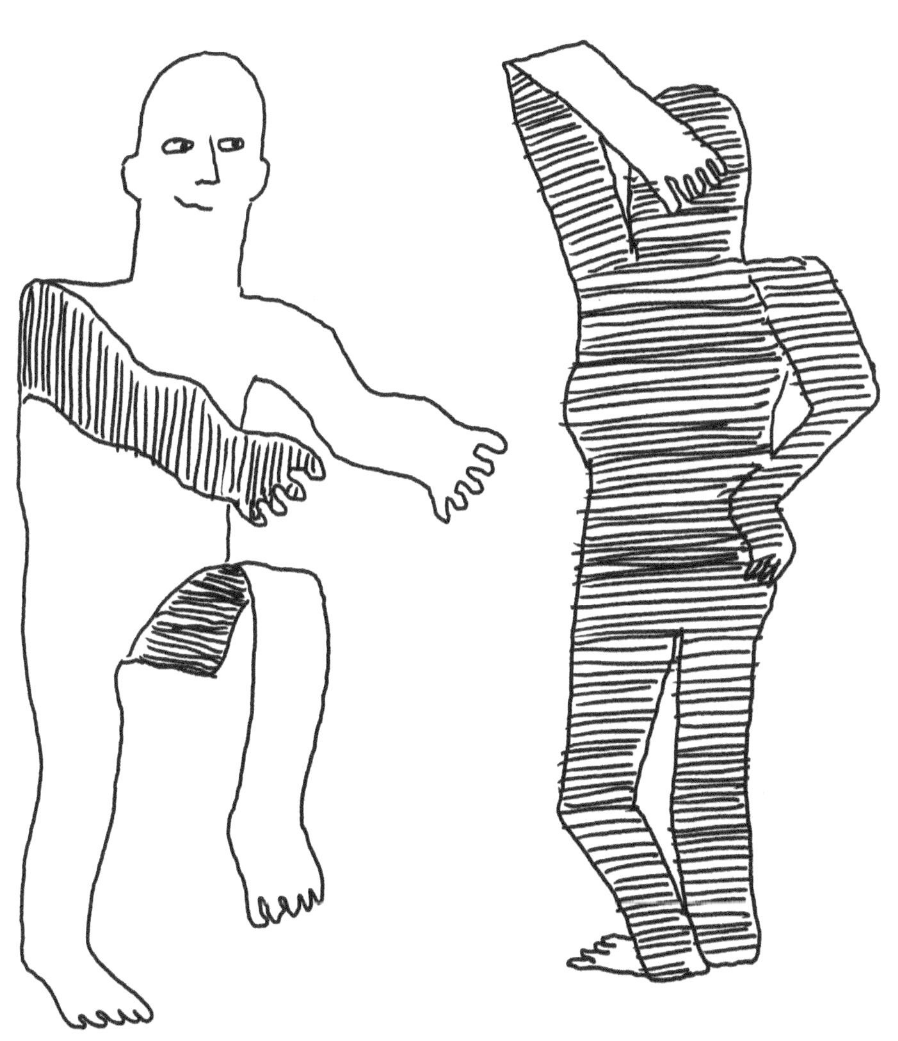

"Those who stand on tiptoes do not stand firmly.
Those who rush ahead don't get very far.
Those who try to outshine others dim their own light."

— Lao Tzu, 24

Democritus said "One man means as much to me as a multitude, and a multitude only as much as one man."

— Seneca, *Letters 7.10*

"Renounce knowledge and your problems will end."

— Lao Tzu, 20

"Let us go to our sleep with joy and gladness;
let us say: I have lived; the course which Fortune set
for me is finished. And if God is pleased to add
another day, we should welcome it with glad hearts.
That man is happiest, and is secure in his own
possession of himself, who can await the morrow
without apprehension. When a man has said: 'I have
lived!', every morning he arises he receives a bonus."

— Seneca, *Letters 12.9*

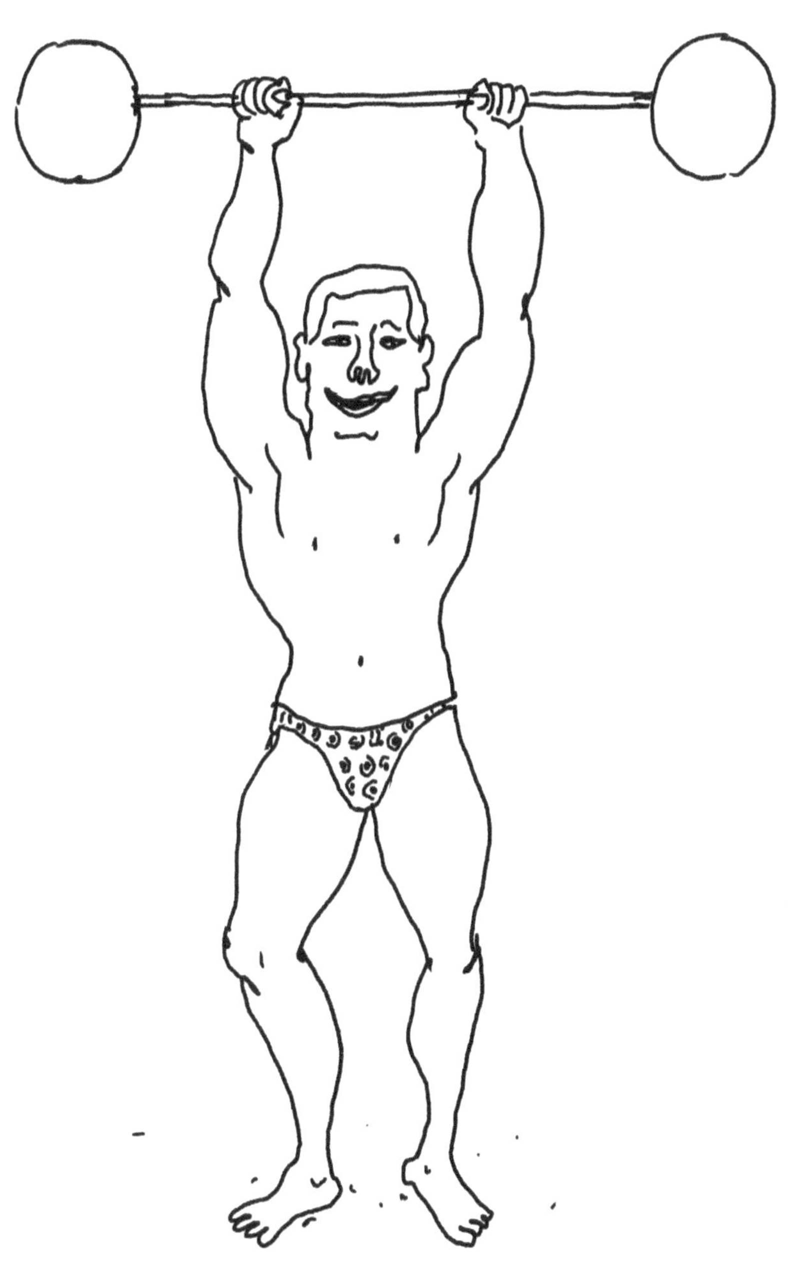

"If rulers could follow the way of the Tao,
  then all of creation would willingly follow their example.
  If selfish desires were to arise after their transformation,
  I would erase them with the power of the Uncarved Block."

— Lao Tzu, 37

"Things themselves don't touch the soul, not in the
  least degree; nor have they admission to the soul,
  nor can they turn or move the soul: but the soul turns
  and moves itself alone, and whatever judgements it may
  think proper to make, it makes for itself about the things
  which present to it."

— Marcus Aurelius, *Meditations, 5.18*

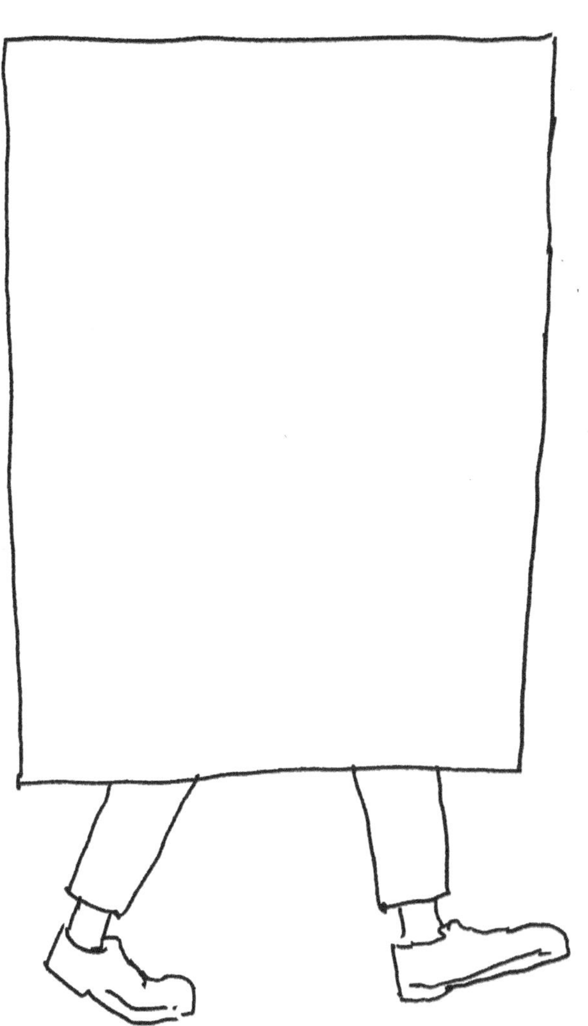

TAO

"The virtue of caution seems like cowardice,
  the pure seems to be polluted,
  the true square seems to have no corners,
  the best vessels take the most time to finish,
  the greatest sounds cannot be heard,
  and the greatest image has no form."

— Lao Tzu, 41

STO

"Show those qualities then which are
  altogether in thy power: sincerity, gravity,
  endurance of labour, aversion to pleasure,
  contentment with thy portion and with few things,
  benevolence, frankness, no love of superfluity,
  freedom from trifling magnanimity."

— Marcus Aurelius, *Meditations, 5.5*

"Those whose desires are few get them,
  those whose desires are great go astray."

— Lao Tzu, 22

"Happy is the man who can make others better, not
  merely when he is in their company, but even when
  he is in their thoughts! And happy also is he who can
  so revere a man as to calm and regulate himself
  by calling him to mind! One who can so revere another,
  will soon be himself worthy of reverence."

— Seneca, *Letters 11.9*

"Those who know others are intelligent;
 those who know themselves are truly wise."

— Lao Tzu, 33

"Suppose any man shall despise me.
 Let him look to that himself. But I will look to this,
 that I be not discovered doing or saying anything
 deserving of contempt. Shall any man hate me?
 Let him look to it. But I will be mild and benevolent
 towards every man, and ready to show even him
 his mistake, not reproachfully, nor yet as making
 a display of my endurance, but nobly and honestly."

— Marcus Aurelius, *Meditations, 11.18*

"The Master's mind is shut off from the world.
Only for the sake of the people does she muddle
her mind. They look to her in anticipation.
Yet she treats them all as her children."

— Lao Tzu, 49

"Judge every word and deed which are according
to nature to be fit for thee; and be not diverted
by the blame which follows from any people nor
by their words, but if a thing is good to be done or said,
do not consider it unworthy of thee."

— Marcus Aurelius, *Meditations, 5.3*

"Those who leave the womb at birth and those who enter
their source at death, of these: three out of ten celebrate
life, three out of ten celebrate death, and three out of ten
simply go from life to death. What is the reason for this?
Because they are afraid of dying, they cannot live."

— Lao Tzu, 50

"What I advise you to do is, not to be unhappy before
the crisis comes; since it may be that the dangers before
which you paled as if they were threatening you, will
never come upon you; they certainly have not yet come."

— Seneca, *Letters 13.4*

"To wear fancy clothes and ornaments,
 to have your fill of food and drink and
 to waste all of your money buying possessions
 is called the crime of excess.
 Oh, how these things go against the way of the Tao!"

— Lao Tzu, 53

"Golden indeed will be the gift with which I shall load
 you; since we have mentioned gold, let me tell you how
 its use and enjoyment may bring you greater pleasure.
 'He who needs riches least, enjoys riches most.'"

— Seneca, *Letters 14.17*

"Those who follow the Tao early
will have an abundance of virtue.
When there is an abundance of virtue,
there is nothing that can not be done."

— Lao Tzu, 59

"Thou sufferest this justly:
for thou choosest rather
to become good tomorrow
than to be good today."

— Marcus Aurelius, *Meditations 8.24*

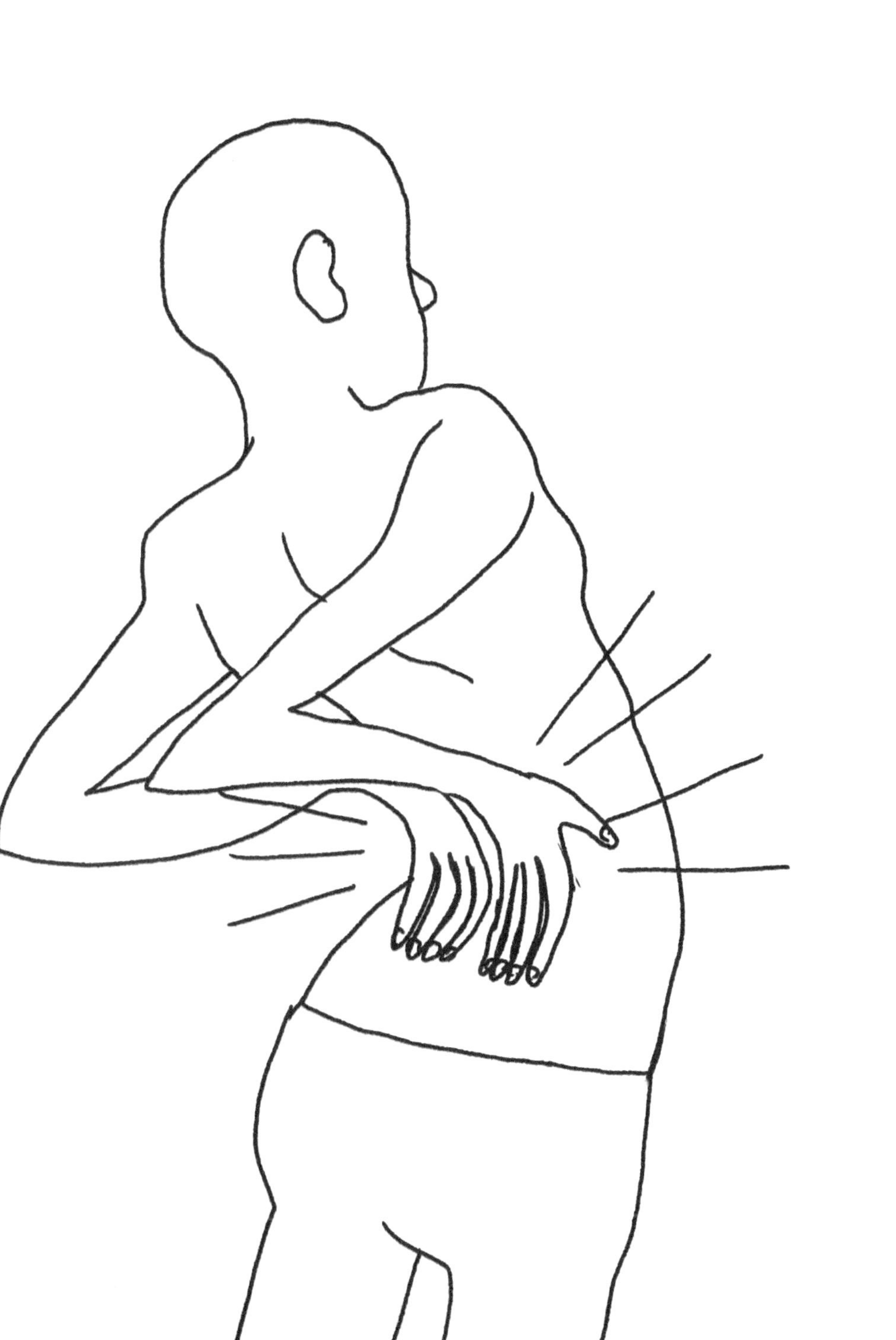

"That which offers no resistance
 can enter where there is no space."

— Lao Tzu, 43

"Wipe out thy imaginations by often saying to thyself:
now it is in my power to let no badness be in this soul,
nor desire nor any perturbation at all; but looking at
all things I see what is their nature, and I use each
according to its value. Remember this power which
thou hast from nature."

— Marcus Aurelius, *Meditations 8.31*

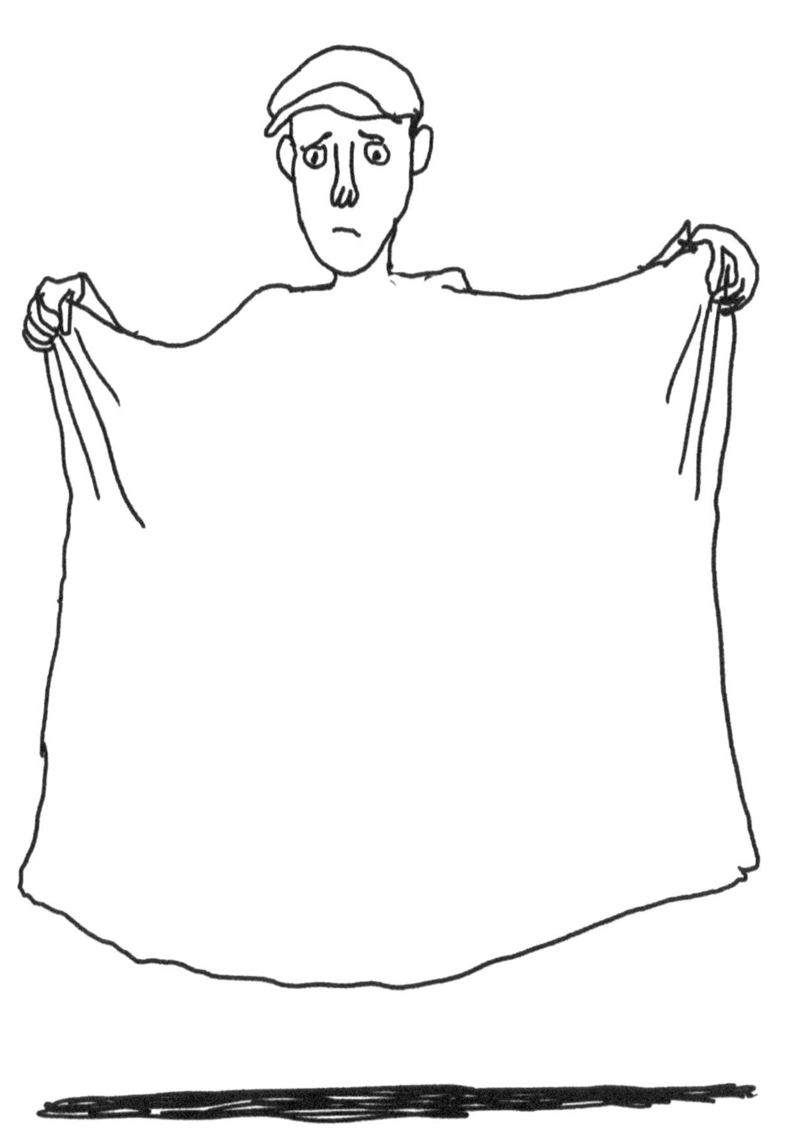

"If you overly esteem talented individuals, people will
become overly competitive. If you overvalue possessions,
people will begin to steal. Do not display your treasures
or people will become envious."

— Lao Tzu, 3

"Speak both in the senate and to every man,
whoever he may be, appropriately,
not with any affectation: use plain discourse."

— Marcus Aurelius, *Meditations 8.32*

"When the world follows the Tao,
 horses run free to fertilize the fields.
 When the world does not follow the Tao,
 war horses are bred outside the cities."

— Lao Tzu, 46

"Away, then, with all excuses like: 'I have not yet enough;
when I have gained the desired amount, then I shall
devote myself wholly to philosophy.' And yet this ideal,
which you are putting off and placing second to other
interests, should be secured first of all; you should
begin with it."

— Seneca, *Letters 17.5*

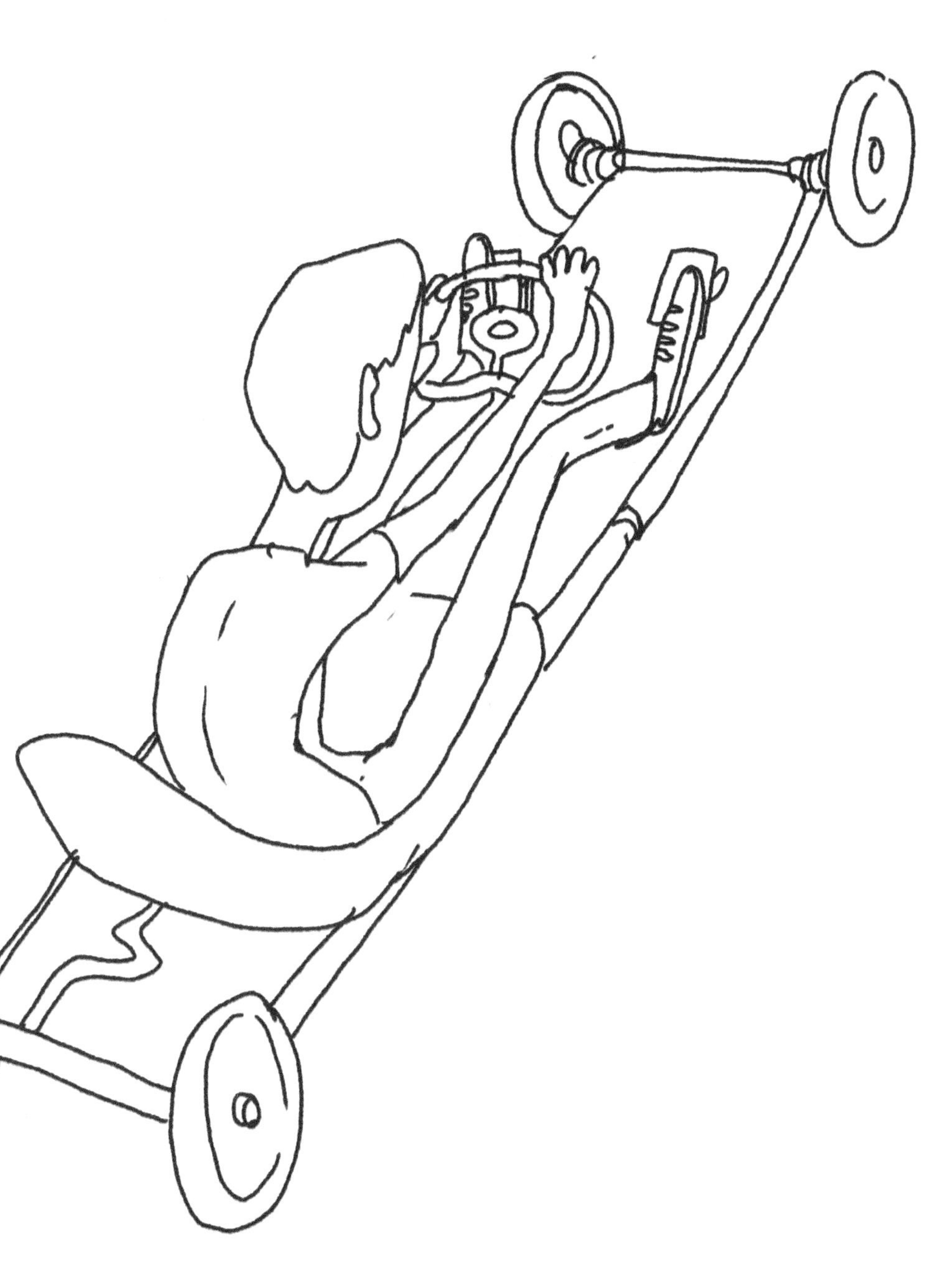

"Those who harm others are like inexperienced boys
 trying to take the place of a great lumberjack.
 Trying to fill his shoes, they will only hurt themselves."

— Lao Tzu, 74

"The outcome of a mighty anger is madness,
 and hence anger should be avoided, not merely that we
 may escape excess, but that we may have a healthy mind."

— Seneca, *Letters 18.15*

"Therefore the Master says: Only he who is the lowest servant of the kingdom, is worthy to become its ruler. He who is willing to tackle the most unpleasant tasks, is the best ruler in the world."

— Lao Tzu, 78

"And if all men refuse to believe that he lives a simple, modest, and contented life, he is neither angry with any of them, nor does he deviate from the way which leads to the end of life, to which a man ought to come pure, tranquil, ready to depart, and without any compulsion perfectly reconciled to his lot."

— Marcus Aurelius, *Meditations 3.16*

TAO

"Forget about knowledge and wisdom,
  and people will be a hundred times better off."

— Lao Tzu, 78

STO

"Nature's wants are slight;
  the demands of opinion are boundless."

— Seneca, *Letters 16.8*

TAO

"The compassionate warrior will be the winner,
  and if compassion is your defense you will be secure.
  Compassion is the protector of Heaven's salvation."

— Lao Tzu, 67

STO

"Speak, and live, in this way;
  see to it that nothing keeps you down."

— Seneca, *Letters 10.4*

JUST TRY IT!

JUNE

Justice

TAO

"Good fortune has its roots in disaster, and disaster lurks
with good fortune. Who knows why these things happen,
or when this cycle will end?"

— Lao Tzu, 58

STO

"We do not put to the test those things which cause our
fear; we do not examine into them; we blench and retreat
just like soldiers who are forced to abandon their camp
because of a dust-cloud raised by stampeding cattle,
or are thrown into a panic by the spreading of some
unauthenticated rumour."

— Seneca, *Letters 13.8*

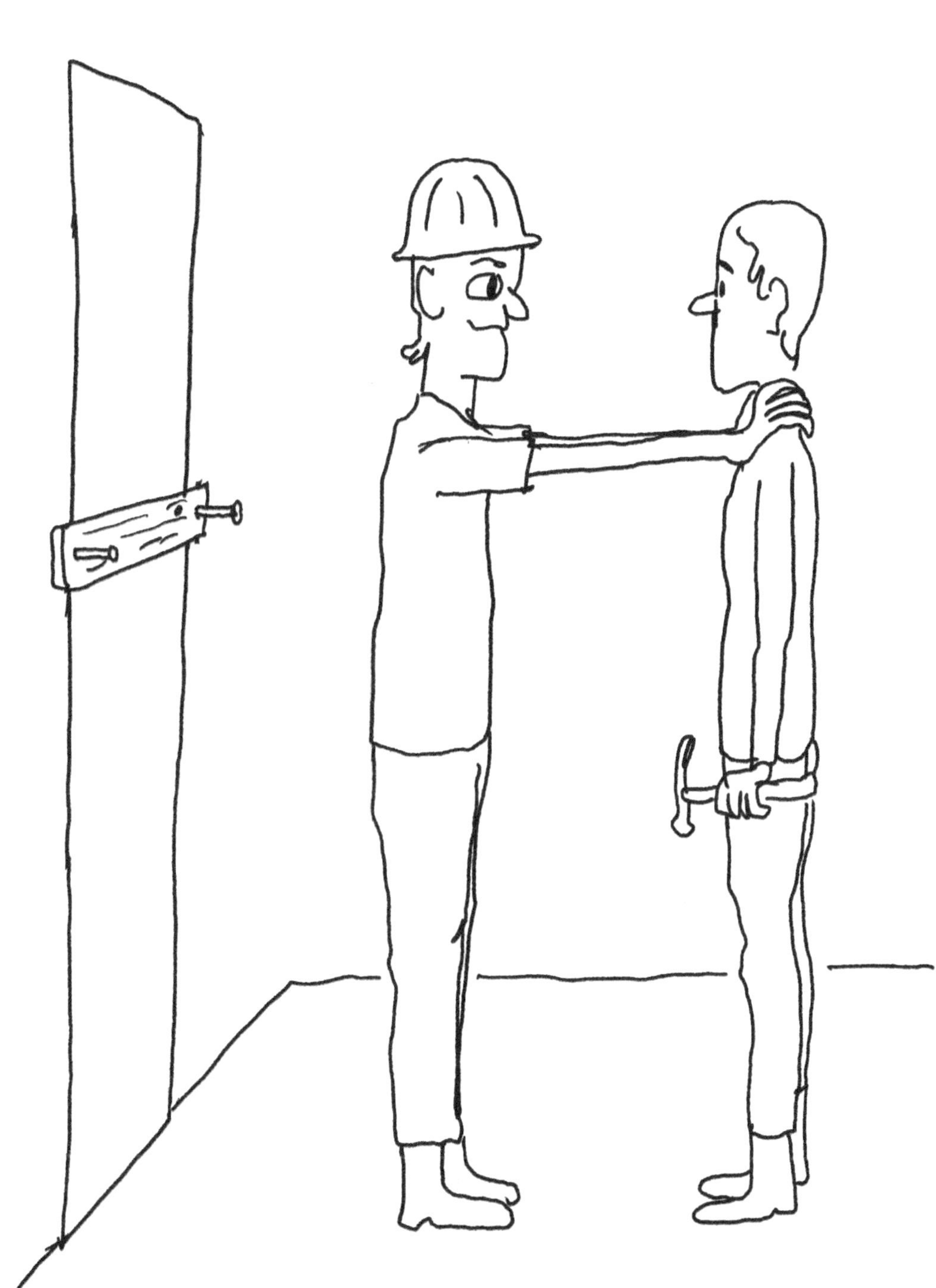

"Freed from desire, you can see the hidden mystery.
By having desire, you can only see what is visibly real."

— Lao Tzu, 1

"By overloading the body with food you strangle the soul
and render it less active. Accordingly, limit the flesh
as much as possible, and allow free play to the spirit."

— Seneca, *Letters 4.2*

"Those who persist will reach their goal.
Those who keep their course have a strong will.
Those who embrace the reality of death
live in the infinite."

— Lao Tzu, 33

"In the morning when thou risest unwillingly,
let this thought be present: I am rising to the work
of a human being. Why then am I dissatisfied if I am
going to do the things for which I exist and for which I
was brought into the world? Or have I been made
for this, to lie in the bed-clothes and keep myself warm?"

— Marcus Aurelius, *Meditations, 5.1*

TAO

"Since the Tao is without wants and desires
it can be considered humble. All of creation
seeks it for refuge, yet it does not seek to master
or control. Because it does not seek greatness
it is able to accomplish truly great things."

— Lao Tzu, 34

STO

"Lay these words to heart, Lucilius, that you may scorn
the pleasure which comes from the applause of the
majority. Many men praise you; but have you any reason
for being pleased with yourself, if you are a person whom
the many can understand? Your good qualities should
face inwards."

— Seneca, *Letters 7.12*

TAO

"The spirit of emptiness is immortal.
It is called the Great Mother
because it gives birth to Heaven and Earth."

— Lao Tzu, 6

STO

"Someone or other was asked what was the object
of all this study applied to an art that would reach
but very few. He replied: I am content with few,
content with one, content with none at all."

— Seneca, *Letters 7.11*

"The sharper the knife the easier it is to dull.
The more wealth you possess the harder
it is to protect. Pride brings its own trouble."

— Lao Tzu, 9

"The acquisition of riches has been for many men
not an end but a change of troubles."

— Seneca, *Letters 17.11*

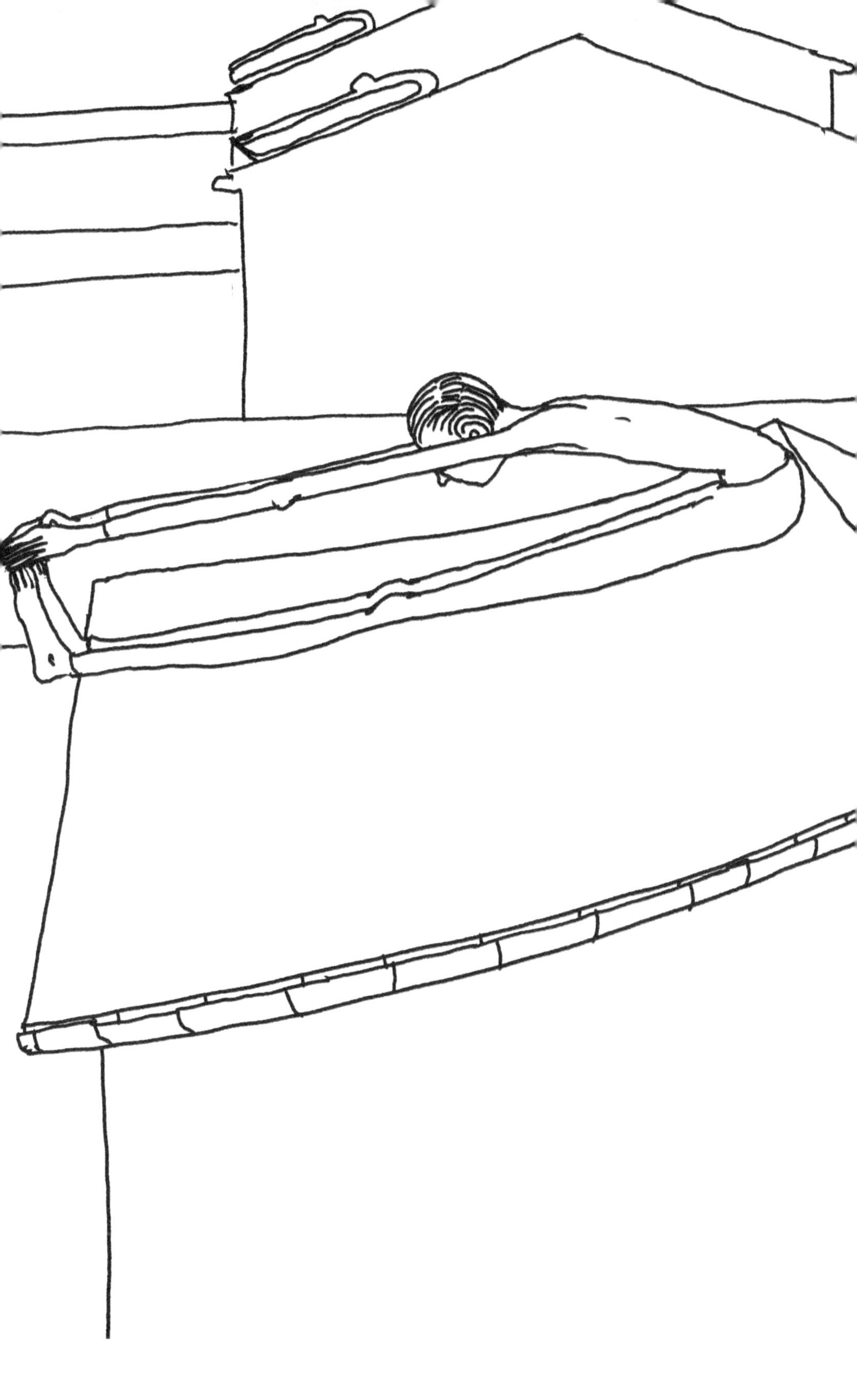

"The greatest virtue you can have comes from
following the Tao, which takes a form that is
intangible and evasive, yet we know it exists.
Intangible and evasive, yet it has a manifestation.
Secluded and dark, yet there is a vitality within it.
Its vitality is very genuine. Within it we can find order."

— Lao Tzu, 9

"If then everything else is common to all, there remains
that which is peculiar to the good man: to be pleased
and content with what happens, and with the thread
which is spun for him; and not to defile the divinity
which is planted in his breast, nor disturb it by a crowd
of images, but to preserve it tranquil, following it
obediently as a god, neither saying anything contrary
to the truth, nor doing anything contrary to justice."

— Marcus Aurelius, *Meditations 3.16*

TAO

"Teaching without words,
 acting without acting,
 the way is realized."

— Lao Tzu, 43

STO

"I do not know any person
 with whom I should prefer you
 to associate rather than yourself."

— Seneca, *Letters 10.2*

"Take care of difficult problems while they are still easy;
do easy things before they become too hard."

— Lao Tzu, 63

"Pacuvius used to hold a regular burial sacrifice in his
own honour, with wine and the usual funeral feasting,
and then would have himself carried from the dining-
room to his chamber, while eunuchs applauded and sang
in Greek to a musical accompaniment: 'He has lived his
life, he has lived his life!' Thus Pacuvius had himself
carried out to burial every day."

— Seneca, *Letters 12.8*

ANY LUCK OVER THERE?
THIS ONE WONT BUDGE.

"The ancient Masters who understood the way of the Tao
did not educate people, but helped them forget."

— Lao Tzu, 65

"In order that you may know that these sentiments
are universal and suggested of course by Nature,
you will find in one of the comic poets this verse:
Unblest is he who thinks himself unblest."

— Seneca, *Letters 12.8*

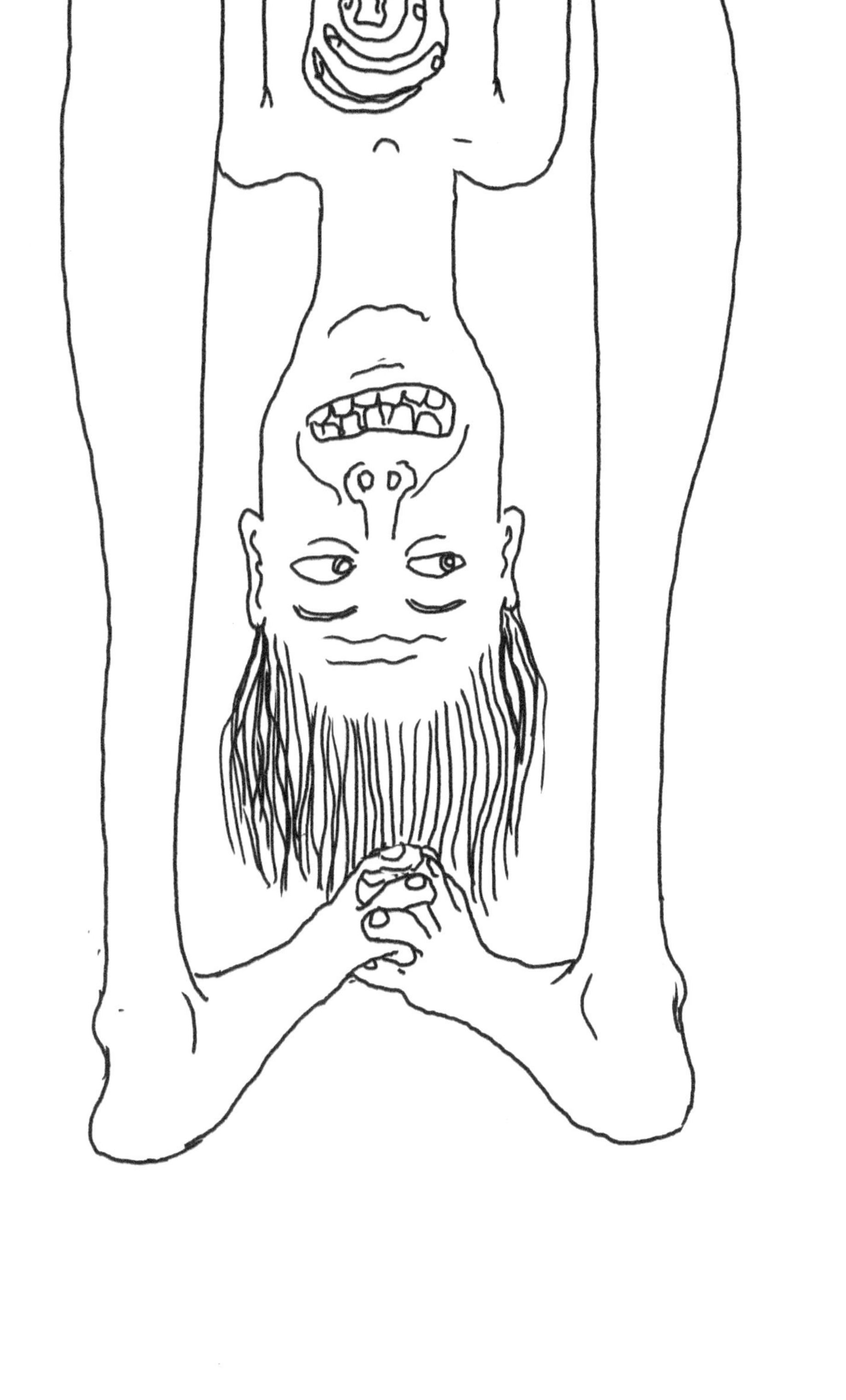

TAO

"The world talks about honoring the Tao,
  but you can't tell it from their actions.
  Because it is thought of as great,
  the world makes light of it.
  It seems too easy for anyone to use."

— Lao Tzu, 67

STO

"The fool, with all his other faults, has this also:
  he is always getting ready to live."

— Seneca, *Letters 13.17*

"With compassion, you will be able to be brave,
 With moderation, you will be able to give to others,
 With humility, you will be able to become a great leader."

— Lao Tzu, 67

"No man can live a happy life,
 or even a supportable life,
 without the study of wisdom."

— Seneca, *Letters 16.1*

"The master trusts people who are trustworthy.
She also trusts people who aren't trustworthy.
This is how she gains true trust."

— Lao Tzu, 49

"Ponder for a long time whether you shall admit a given
person to your friendship; but when you have decided
to admit him, welcome him with all your heart and soul.
Speak as boldly with him as with yourself."

— Seneca, *Letters 3.2*

"The master seeks no possessions. She learns by
unlearning, thus she is able to understand all things.
This gives her the ability to help all of creation. "

— Lao Tzu, 64

"Socrates said to one who was reminding him to prepare
for his trial, 'Do you not think then that I have been
preparing for it all my life? By what kind of preparation?
I have maintained that which was in my own power.'"

— Epictetus, *Book 2, Discourses, Book 2, 2.1*

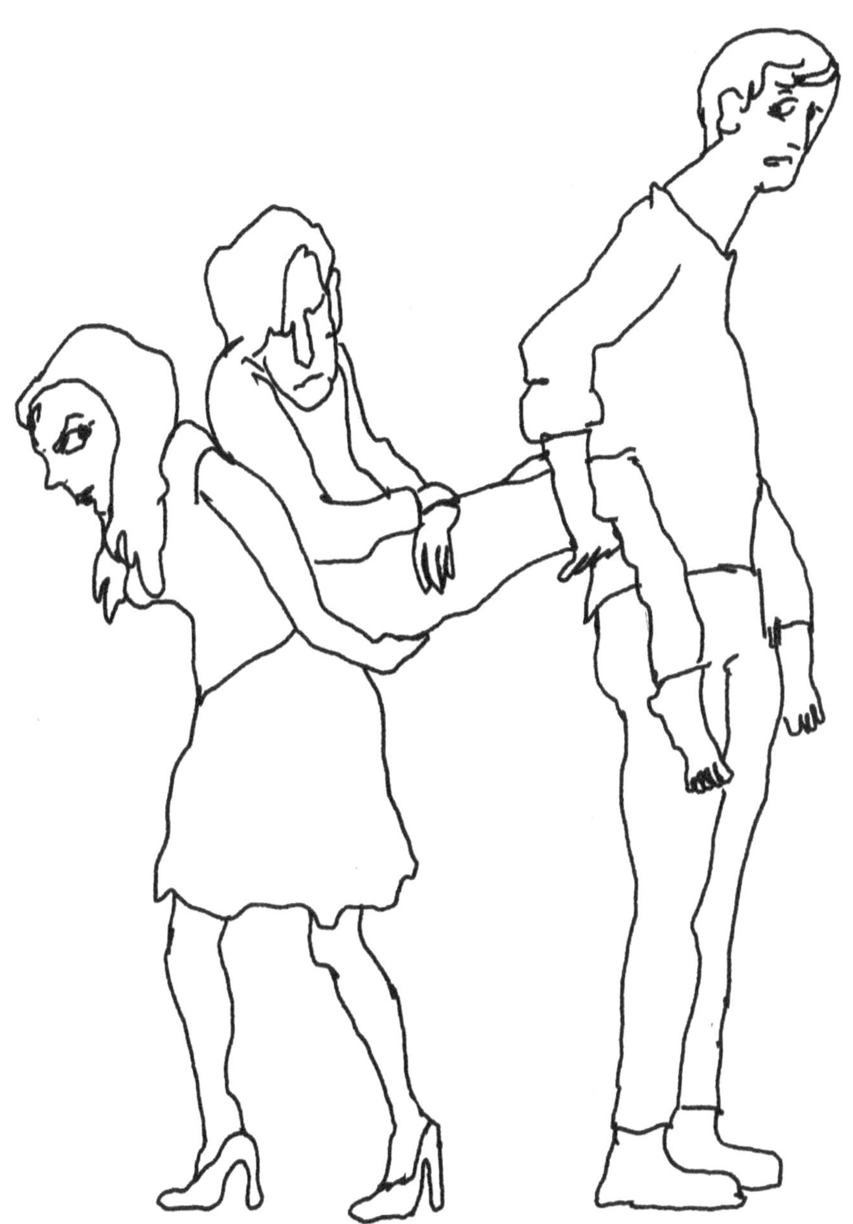

"Good things seem to change into bad,
 and bad things often turn out for good.
 These things have always been hard to comprehend."

— Lao Tzu, 58

"It is likely that some troubles will befall us;
 but it is not a present fact.
 How often has the unexpected happened!
 How often has the expected never come to pass!
 And even though it is ordained to be,
 what does it avail to run out to meet your suffering?
 You will suffer soon enough, when it arrives;
 so look forward meanwhile to better things."

— Seneca, *Letters 13.10*

"There is no greater crime
than encouraging selfish desires,
and no greater misfortune than greed."

— Lao Tzu, 46

"Fix a limit which you will not even desire to pass,
should you have the power. At last, then, away with
all these treacherous goods! They look better to those
who hope for them than to those who have attained
them. If there were anything substantial in them,
they would sooner or later satisfy you; as it is,
they merely rouse the drinkers' thirst."

— Seneca, *Letters 15.11*

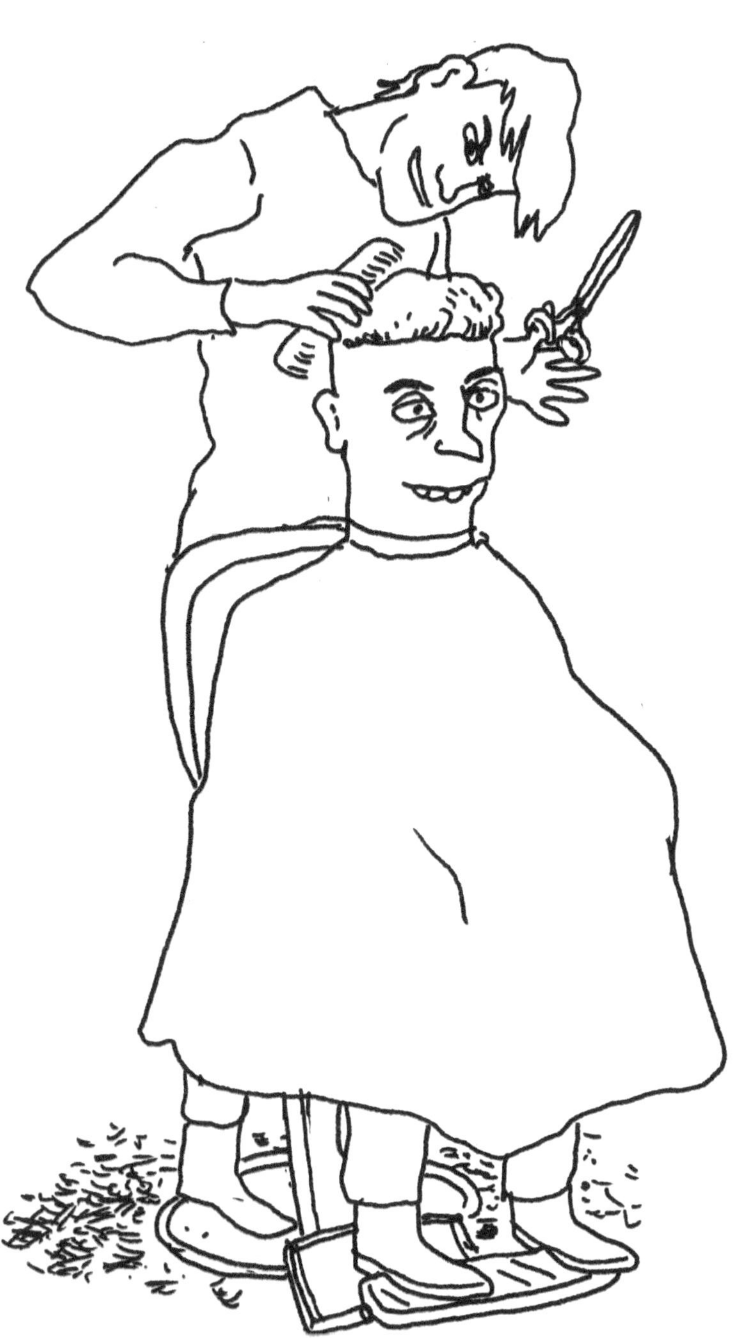

"The greatest accomplishments seem imperfect,
yet their usefulness is not diminished.
The greatest fullness seems empty,
yet it will be inexhaustible."

— Lao Tzu, 45

"Why, then, should you reject Philosophy as a comrade?
Even the rich man copies her ways
when he is in his senses.
If you wish to have leisure for your mind,
either be a poor man, or resemble a poor man.
Study cannot be helpful unless you take pains
to live simply; and living simply is voluntary poverty."

— Seneca, *Letters 17.5*

"Humanity follows the Earth. Earth follows Heaven.
Heaven follows the Tao. The Tao follows only itself."

— Lao Tzu, 25

"Natural desires are limited; but those which spring
from false opinion can have no stopping-point.
The false has no limits. When you are travelling
on a road, there must be an end; but when astray,
your wanderings are limitless. Recall your steps,
therefore, from idle things, and when you would
know whether that which you seek is based upon
a natural or upon a misleading desire,
consider whether it can stop at any definite point.
If you find, after having travelled far, that there is
a more distant goal always in view, you may be sure
that this condition is contrary to nature."

— Seneca, *Letters 17.5*

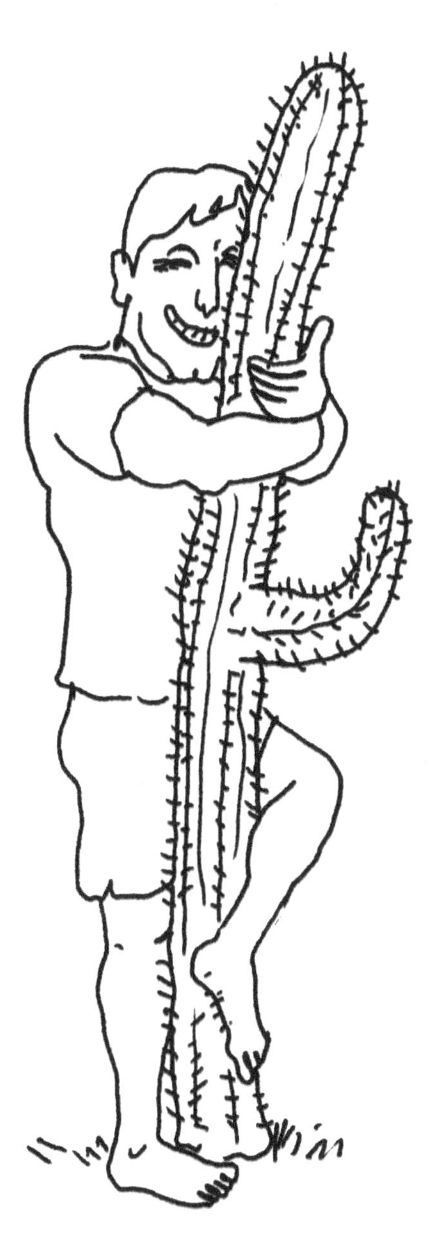

TAO

"If you are as concerned about the outcome
 as you are about the beginning,
 then it is hard to do things wrong."

— Lao Tzu, 64

STO

"If anything forbids you to live nobly,
 nothing forbids you to die nobly."

— Seneca, *Letters 17.5*

"Everyone knows that the soft and yielding
overcomes the rigid and hard, but few
can put this knowledge into practice."

— Lao Tzu, 78

"Pain is either an evil to the body - then let the body say
what it thinks of it - or to the soul; but it is in the power
of the soul to maintain its own serenity and tranquility,
and not to think that pain is an evil. For every judgement
and movement and desire and aversion is within,
and no evil ascends so high."

— Marcus Aurelius, *Meditations 8.30*

TAO

"The block of wood is carved into utensils by carving
  space into the wood. The Master uses the utensils,
  but prefers to keeps the block uncarved
  because of its limitless possibilities."

— Lao Tzu, 28

STO

"If thou workest at that which is before thee,
  following right reason seriously, vigorously, calmly,
  without allowing anything else to distract thee,
  but keeping thy divine part pure, as if thou
  shouldst be bound to give it back immediately;
  if thou holdest to this, expecting nothing,
  fearing nothing, but satisfied with thy present
  activity according to nature, and with heroic truth
  in every word and sound which thou utterest,
  thou wilt live happy. And there is no man
  who is able to prevent this."

— Marcus Aurelius, *Meditations 3.12*

IT'S A
CONVERSATION
PIECE

"The Tao never acts with force,
 yet there is nothing that it can not do."

— Lao Tzu, 37

"Different things delight different people.
 But it is my delight to keep the ruling faculty sound
 without turning away either from any man
 or from any of the things which happen to men,
 but looking at and receiving all with welcome eyes
 and using everything according to its value."

— Marcus Aurelius, *Meditations 8.40*

"When the Tao is forgotten, there is righteousness.
 When righteousness is forgotten, there is morality.
 When morality is forgotten, there are rituals.
 Rituals are the husk of faith
 and the beginning of confusion."

— Lao Tzu, 38

"Many of our troubles may be explained
 from the fact that we live according to a pattern,
 and, instead of arranging our lives according to reason,
 are led astray by convention."

— Seneca, *Letters 12*

"Which is more important, your honor or your life?
 Which is more valuable, your possessions or your person?
 Which is more destructive, success or failure?
 Because of this, great love extracts a great cost
 and true wealth requires greater loss."

— Lao Tzu, 44

"Away with fripperies which only serve for show!
 As to what the future's uncertain lot has in store,
 why should I demand of Fortune that she give,
 rather than demand of myself that I should not crave?
 And why should l crave? Shall I heap up my winnings,
 and forget that man's lot is unsubstantial?
 For what end should I toil?
 Lo, to-day is the last; if not, it is near the last."

— Seneca, *Letters 15.11*

"When we know we are the Mother's child,
  we begin to guard the qualities of the Mother in us.
  She will protect us from all danger
  even if we lose our life."

— Lao Tzu, 52

"I go through the things which happen
  according to nature until I shall fall and rest,
  breathing out my breath into that element
  out of which I daily draw it in, and falling upon
  that earth out of which my father collected the seed,
  and my mother the blood, and my nurse the milk;
  out of which during so many years I have been supplied
  with food and drink; which bears me when I tread on it
  and abuse it for so many purposes."

— Marcus Aurelius, *Meditations 5.4*

"If this idea is cultivated in the individual,
  then virtue will become genuine.
  If this idea is cultivated in the family,
  then virtue in the family will be great.
  If this idea is cultivated in the community,
  then virtue will go a long way.
  If this idea is cultivated in the country,
  then virtue will be in many places.
  If this idea is cultivated in the world,
  then virtue will be with everyone."

— Lao Tzu, 52

"Cultivate that good which improves with the years."

— Seneca, *Letters 15.5*

"Without unity, the sky becomes filthy.
Without unity, the earth becomes unstable.
Without unity, the spirits become unresponsive
and disappear. Without unity, the valleys
become dry as a desert. Without unity,
humankind can't reproduce and becomes extinct.
Without unity, our leaders become corrupt and fall."

— Lao Tzu, 39

"Epicurus said 'Whoever does not regard what he has
as most ample wealth, is unhappy, though he be master
of the whole world.' Or, if the following seems to you
a more suitable phrase - for we must try to render
the meaning and not the mere words -
'A man may rule the world and still be unhappy,
if he does not feel that he is supremely happy.'"

— Seneca, *Letters 9.20*

"The people will not feel burdened,
 if a wise person is in a position of power.
 The people will not feel like they are being manipulated,
 if a wise person is in front as their leader.
 The whole world will ask for her guidance,
 and will never get tired of her."

— Lao Tzu, 26

"The man who is honest and good ought to be exactly like
 a man who smells strong, so that the bystander as soon
 as he comes near him must smell whether he choose
 or not. The good and simple and benevolent show all
 these things in the eyes, and there is no mistaking."

— Marcus Aurelius, *Meditations 11.20*

MAMMA?

"If the Tao is used to govern the world,
  then evil will lose its power to harm the people.
  Not because evil will no longer exist,
  but because it has lost its power."

— Lao Tzu, 60

"There will be many happenings which will serve
  to postpone, or end, or pass on to another person,
  the trials which are near or even in your very presence.
  A fire has opened the way to flight. Men have been
  let down softly by a catastrophe. Sometimes the sword
  has been checked even at the victim's throat.
  Men have survived their own executioners.
  Even bad fortune is fickle. Perhaps it will come,
  perhaps not; in the meantime it is not.
  So look forward to better things."

— Seneca, *Letters 13.11*

"Thirty spokes are joined together in a wheel, but it
is the center hole that allows the wheel to function.
We fashion wood for a house, but it is the emptiness
inside that makes it livable. We work with the
substantial, but the emptiness is what we use."

— Lao Tzu, 11

"Games also will be useful: for moderate pleasure
relieves the mind and brings it to a proper balance."

— Seneca, *Dialogues Of Anger, 2.20.4*

POSTSCRIPT

ACKNOWLEDGEMENTS

Our Wives

ATTRIBUTIONS

**All quotes were sourced and/or adapted from the following works
in the public domain:**

The Discourses of Epictetus; with the Encheiridion and Fragments
by Epictetus; translated from Koine Greek by George Long, 1877
https://en.wikisource.org/wiki/The_Discourses_of_Epictetus;_with_the_
Encheiridion_and_Fragments

Lives of Eminent Philosophers by Diogenes Laërtius, 1925
https://penelope.uchicago.edu/Thayer/E/Roman/Texts/Diogenes_Laertius/home.
html

Meditations of Marcus Aurelius; translated by George Long, 1890
https://classics.mit.edu/Antoninus/meditations.html

Minor Dialogs Together with the Dialog "On Clemency" by Seneca;
translated by Aubrey Stewart, 1900
https://en.wikisource.org/wiki/Of_Peace_of_Mind

Moral letters to Lucilius (Epistulae morales ad Lucilium) by Seneca;
translated by Richard Mott Gummere, 1917, 1920, 1925
https://en.wikisource.org/wiki/Moral_letters_to_Lucilius

Tao Te Ching by Lao-Tzu; translated by J.H.Mcdonald, 1996
https://faculty.mnsu.edu/scottgr/wp-content/uploads/sites/34/2014/08/TaoTeChing.
pdf

The Thoughts Of The Emperor Marcus Aurelius Antoninus by Marcus Aurelius
Antoninus; translated from Koine Greek by George Long, 1862
https://en.wikisource.org/wiki/The_Thoughts_of_the_Emperor_Marcus_Aurelius_
Antoninus

The Works of Epictetus. Consisting of His Discourses, in Four Books,
The Enchiridion, and Fragments. A Translation from the Greek based on
that of Elizabeth Carter, 1758; by Thomas Wentworth Higginson, 1865
https://oll-resources.s3.us-east-2.amazonaws.com/oll3/store/titles/1477/
Epictetus_0755_EBk_v6.0.pdf

S TO
WHAT ?

(THIS PAGE LEFT INTENTIONALLY BLANK - FEEL FREE)

[illegible signature]